I0555025

Why Baptize Babies?

An Explanation of the Theology
and Practice of the Reformed Churches

Mark Horne

Why Baptize Babies?
An Explanation of the Theology and
Practice of the Reformed Churches
by Mark Horne

Copyright © 2007, 2023 Mark Horne
Athanasius Press
715 Cypress Street
West Monroe, Louisiana, 71291
www.athanasiuspress.org

Cover design and typesetting: Rachel Rosales

ISBN: 978-1-957726-03-8

Printed in the United States of America.

Quick Reference

Introduction

Anyone who visits a church in the reformed tradition will learn sooner or later that the children in these churches are commonly baptized quite soon after they are born. Of course, many people know that liberal mainline churches baptize children, and many are aware that non-Protestant churches baptize babies as well. Some realize that Lutheran or Episcopal denominations baptize babies and assume this is because these traditions didn't quite break free from the grip of Roman Catholic traditionalism, but the fact is that sincere *Bible-believing, inerrancy-affirming* evangelical churches also baptize babies.

Babies are too young to give any sort of outward profession of faith, yet reformed or Presbyterian ministers baptize them into the name of the Father, Son, and Holy Spirit. They do not baptize infants *merely* because they are sentimentally attached to them, nor because that is what was traditionally done in the history of the church.

Of course, reformed or Presbyterian pastors *are* sentimentally attached to their children, as are we all, and there is very little doubt that all the way back to the apostolic age the church has always baptized the children of Christians. Nevertheless, as powerful as those reasons are, they are not the reason that we practice paedobaptism ("baptism of infants"). We practice paedobaptism because we are convinced beyond a shadow of a doubt that the Bible teaches us to do so.

Many other Bible-believing Christians, however, are sure that the Bible does *not* teach paedobaptism. On the contrary, they think only those who verbally and convincingly profess faith in Jesus should be baptized. Indeed, conservative reformed congregations are often visited by Christians from good churches—who hold to the Scriptures of the Old and New Testaments as infallible Word of God and the final authority for all of life—who also think that paedobaptism is unbiblical. They are convinced that the only proper recipients of baptism are those who have made a credible profession of faith in a way that is only possible when a person has reached a certain age. All such believers are our brothers and sisters in Christ, and we are glad to have them among us. The Baptist tradition, whether that is in their official denominational name or not, has done much good in North America. When Christians disagree, they must do so in a Christian manner, and hopefully this small book will assist in facilitating peaceful discussion.

Perhaps you are one of these people who believes—and has always been taught—that one must first reach a certain age and make a profession of faith before being baptized. If so, this is written for you. It is written not so much to change your mind as it is to show you the way *our* minds work and to answer the question, "How is it that reformed Christians *both* believe the Bible *and* practice paedobaptism?" There are many cults out there, after all, which claim to believe the Bible as the Word of God, yet these false religions reject the true God by denying key doctrines like the Trinity or the Incarnation. You have a right to ask to be assured that our claim of loyalty to Scripture is not some sort of game, but rather a sincere attempt to submit to the authority of God's Word. You may not agree with us, but this is written so that you will at least know where we are coming from.

Prooftexting vs. Proving from the Text

The first thing which usually comes up in a discussion of paedobaptism versus credobaptism ("believer's baptism") is the claim that there is no verse which authorizes the baptism of babies in the New Testament. This claim requires some examination.

If anyone were to reduce his or her beliefs to only what is *directly and explicitly stated* in the Bible, then he would not be a Christian at all, but a cult member. The simple fact of the matter is that essential doctrines such as that of the Trinity or Christ's two natures are not *formulated* for us in the New Testament. Rather, those doctrines developed in the history of the church through careful study of the Scripture, reflection, and application, so that a formulation was constructed which applied biblical principles and did no injustice to any of the Bible's explicit teachings. Likewise, our practice of baptism must not do injustice to any teaching of Scripture, and moreover it must apply or extend biblical practices and principles.

Paedobaptism Is Not Prohibited

Obviously, if there is some explicit statement in Scripture that only those who profess faith are to be baptized, then paedobaptism is wrong, but there is no such text. Reformed and Presbyterian Christians also believe that no unbeliever should be baptized until he or she repents and professes faith in Christ. Thus, we are entirely comfortable with the statements requiring faith and repentance to accompany baptism (Mark 16:16; Acts 2:38). We would make those same statements in those same situations. We too believe that all non-Christians must repent and believe the Gospel before they are baptized into Christ and his church.

But are the children of believers included in such statements? Must children also repent and verbally articulate their faith in order to receive baptism? We would have to answer that question "yes" if we are to accept these verses requiring repentance as prooftexts against paedobaptism. Consider this. When Paul wrote, "If anyone is not willing to work, let him not eat" (2 Thess. 3:10b), we take it for granted he was not referring to babies. We do not expect infants to work for their supper. We interpret the verse according to what we understand to be its intended scope. Just as we think Paul was referring only to able-bodied adults when he wrote to the Thessalonians about the requirement that Christians work, so Presbyterians believe the passages requiring an outward profession of faith and repentance are referring to relatively mature converts to the faith.

We may be wrong, but one can't simply quote passages about adult converts and assume that they end all discussion. It is only because someone already assumes that babies should not be baptized that he understands such passages exclude infants from baptism. The question still needs to be answered: is such an assumption justified from Scripture?

Paedobaptism Is Commanded

There *are* New Testament prooftexts for paedobaptism. The problem is that credobaptists do not accept the paedobaptist interpretation of those texts. If we want to be persuasive, we will have to do more work digging through all of Scripture to demonstrate how those texts are to be interpreted. Thus, we will deal with these passages later in this book after we've done some deeper searching through the Bible.

Credobaptism Is Not Commanded

Furthermore, there is *no* New Testament prooftext to support the practice of delaying baptism until the child of a believer has reached a certain level of maturity, understanding, or ability to make a profession of faith. Nowhere in the New Testament do we read of any case in which the child of believers is baptized after he has reached a certain age. Nor do we find any instruction whatsoever in any of the epistles as to how old the child of believers must be or what sort of criteria he must meet in order to be baptized. There is not a hint in the New Testament that children are expected to go through such a rite at a particular age. All "believer's baptisms" mentioned in the New Testament involve adult converts from Judaism or paganism. The entire current cultural idea of children reaching an "age of accountability," "asking Jesus into their hearts," and then getting baptized is simply foreign to the New Testament record. The New Testament contains neither any examples of nor any instructions concerning children of Christians being treated in this manner.

The Word Of God Encompasses More Than The New Testament

Finally, if there were no paedobaptist prooftexts in the New Testament, that would not mean that there is no such prooftext in *Scripture*. After all, the New Testament only makes up about a quarter of the whole Bible. Many things changed with the work of Christ, but not everything. To put it another way, many things changed *in the church*. Our belief in paedobaptism has much to do with our belief that the church of Jesus Christ began in Genesis with God separating a people from the nations. This same church continued on through different stages in history as one continuous people of God, and still continues on today. The work of Christ was the most radical change in the church, but it is still the same church. We belong to the same institution as Seth, Noah, Abraham, Moses, David, and Ezekiel. Any discussion of baptism which ignores this vast heritage and its authoritative expression in the Word of God is bound to be distorted. It is to this heritage that we will now turn to consider.

Understanding
the Covenant

Adam and Eve were created "very good" (Gen. 1:31). Furthermore, they were told to have many children and to take dominion over the world (Gen. 1:28). They were also given a special Garden in which to live, with a special Tree of Life from which to eat (Gen. 1:9, 16).

Here's a question to ponder. Had the fall not occurred, would the children of Adam and Eve have needed to be converted to God at some point in their lives? The answer is obvious: of course not! Adam and Eve's children would have shared in the blessings God gave to them. Particularly, they would have been born in the same Garden and had the same access to the Tree of Life that their parents had been given. The whole point of the creation account is to show that God made *all* things good—including humanity. Newborn children would not have apprehended God with the same maturity as their parents, but they would have been in the same loving relationship with God that their parents possessed. Remember, in the Bible there is no neutrality. You either love God or you hate God. The idea of "neutral," "amoral" children who have not reached an "age of accountability" is simply alien to the teaching of Scripture. To be "good" is to be right with God. Children would have been conceived and born at peace with God.

It is true, of course, that throughout their lives they would always need to learn more about God and know him better. It is also true that, in their early years, it would have been the parents' responsibility to teach their children about their Lord, but the point is if things continued in the Garden as they had been created, and Adam and Eve had not sinned, then there would be no separate "conversion" required of children so that they would belong to the Lord. The children would belong to the Lord from conception onward. Just as Adam was *created* in a right relationship with God and counted as righteous before he had done *any* works, so his and Eve's children would have been conceived in right standing with God. They would have been righteous in God's sight from the first moment they came to exist.

Sin and Children

Tragically, however, Adam and Eve never bothered to partake of God's gift of the Tree of Life because they lusted after the forbidden fruit of the Tree of the Knowledge of Good and Evil. They sinned against God and fell under his wrath and curse (Gen. 3). They were driven from the Garden of Eden so that neither they nor their children could ever gain access to the Tree of Life. They did not fall for themselves alone. Just as their children would have enjoyed the benefits and blessings of Adam's obedience and perseverance in God's unmerited favor, so also the children suffered the corruption and guilt of Adam's sin. Adam's children were born in his image as sinners (Gen. 5:3). By Adam's sin, death and sin spread to all people because we all sinned in him (Rom. 5:12–14).

All children are conceived and born as sinners. They are not conceived and born as innocents who later sin. "Behold I was brought forth in iniquity, and in sin my mother conceived me" (Ps. 58:3). Again, there is no "age of accountability" or "age of innocence." It is true that the Bible talks about those too young to have knowledge of good and evil (Deut. 1:39), but these "children" include nineteen-year-olds (Num. 14:29). The knowledge spoken of in those passages does not refer to the ability to sin, but rather to the ability to make certain judgments which require maturity and impose a greater degree of responsibility. We can prove from this that the sins of children are not nearly *as serious* as those of older people, but not that they aren't still serious enough to merit an eternity separated from a holy God. The plain, if mysterious, fact is that babies sin. That is why we live in a world where children die: a curse for sin that would not happen if children were not guilty before God.

The Covenant of Grace

Praise be to God! He did not leave humanity in guilt and sin, under the curse of death, but provided a redemption. He did not destroy Adam and Eve even though they deserved to die. Furthermore, he covered their shameful nakedness by clothing them himself. We know hardly any details of the relationship between God and his people in that earlier period—except for the all-important fact that he indeed had a relationship with a people whom were indeed his. We know this because we read of Abel offering the Lord an acceptable sacrifice, and after Cain killed him, Seth led the people who "began to call upon the name of the Lord" (Gen. 4:26).

As history unfolds for us in Scripture, this relationship is revealed more and more clearly. God calls this relationship a *covenant* which he makes with Noah as a second "Adam" in a new creation (Gen. 8:20–9:11). After Noah's descendants were divided into nations (Gen. 11:1–9), God called Abraham and made a covenant with him so that he would bring salvation to these nations (Gen. 12:1–3, 15, 17). The covenant with Abraham is eventually transfigured into the covenant with Israel given by Moses on Mount Sinai. This covenant developed further through the period of monarchy, and then during and after the exile in Babylon. Finally, Christ transfigured all the preceding covenants, establishing the new covenant in his blood (Matt. 26:28; Luke 22:20; Heb. 9:11–18).

This one covenant of grace is nothing less than salvation. God's "everlasting covenant" is "to be God to you" (Gen. 17:7), to confer "forgiveness of sins" (Matt. 26:28), and to "purify our conscience from dead works to serve the living God" (Heb. 9:14).

Who Are the Members of the Covenant?

For any loving parent, there is an important issue that needs to be addressed: what about our children? Without God's grace, our children, as we just saw, are conceived and born as hell-bound sinners. Does God give us any hope for them?

Yes! God promised Abraham "to be God to you *and to your offspring after you*" (Gen. 17:7). The psalmist reiterates this foundational promise, singing: "But the steadfast love of the Lord is from everlasting to everlasting on those who fear him, and his righteousness to children's children" (Ps. 103:17). "And as for me, this is my covenant with them," says the Lord: "My Spirit that is upon you, and my words that I have put in your mouth, shall not depart out of your mouth, or out of the mouth of your offspring, or out of the mouth of your children's offspring," says the Lord, "from this time forth and forevermore" (Isa. 59:21).

God doesn't say through Isaiah that his Spirit and Word *will be put* in the mouths of a Christian's grandchildren, but rather that they "will not depart from" them. Obviously, this passage does not discount the fact that all children are born sinners, but it does seem to promise more than the bare hope of a future conversion experience.

When Moses renewed the covenant with Israel, just before he died, he stated emphatically: "It is not with you alone that I am making this sworn covenant, but with whoever is standing here with us today before the Lord our God, and with whoever is not here with us today" (Deut. 29:14–15). And who else was involved in the covenant besides those present with Moses? Moses himself tells us that "the things that are revealed belong to us and *to our children forever*, that we may do all the words of this law" (Deut. 29:29). This is not some sort of "external" covenant, for Moses promises that "the Lord your God will circumcise your heart and the heart of your offspring, so that you will love the Lord your God with all your heart and with all your soul, that you may live" (Deut. 30:6).

The bottom line here is that the Bible promises believers regarding their children that God will be their God, that he will give them his righteousness, that his Spirit will not depart from them, and that they are included in his covenant. What more could anybody ask for? Our children are clearly promised eternal salvation. They are declared to be Christians, nothing less.

The expectation that the children of believers are also believers—even while they are in the womb—found its way into the inspired hymns of Israel's worship: "Out of the mouth of babies and infants, you have established strength" (Ps. 8:2). And again: "For you, O Lord, are my hope, my trust, O Lord, from my youth. Upon you I have leaned from before my birth; you are he who took me from my mother's womb. My praise is continually of you . . . O God, from my youth you have taught me" (Ps. 71:5–6, 17). "Yet you are he who took me from the womb; you made me trust you at my mother's breasts. On you was I cast from my birth, and from my mother's womb you have been my God." (Ps. 22:9–10). There are many Christian contemporary hymns today about adult conversion from unbelief, yet there is not one psalm in the Scriptures that speaks of that subject. On the other hand, have you ever sung a hymn that called for you to put yourself in the place of one who was regenerated in the womb? The fact that such lyrics were part of the public corporate worship of Israel strongly indicates that the people of God regarded the salvation of their children from the womb as a perfectly normal and expected event.

The truth is clear: God wants Christians to regard their *children* as Christians. This does not mean they will automatically go to heaven whether or not they continue to believe the gospel. Just like all older Christians, children must continue in the faith, but the point is that children are not little unbelievers who need to be converted. They are not enemies of Christ. They are believers who need to be discipled and encouraged to grow in grace and maturity throughout their whole lives. We can teach them to sing "Jesus Loves Me" and to address God as "Father" when they pray the Lord's Prayer because we possess God's promise that they are our brothers and sisters in Christ.

The Baptism of Children

With the covenant promises came the ceremonial means by which children were placed in God's care. God commanded Abraham that every son was to be circumcised and thus constituted a member of his chosen people (Gen. 17:9–14).

Furthermore, under the Mosaic covenant, not only were infant boys circumcised but all children were cleansed whenever they became defiled. We know this because they were permitted to eat the sanctuary meals. At one point Pharaoh would have let the Israelites go to worship God if they had left their children behind, but Moses had a different idea: "We will go with our young and our old. We will go with our sons and daughters and with our flocks and herds, for *we must hold a feast to the Lord*" (Ex. 10:9). The flocks and herds were needed for sacrifice (Ex. 10:25), but obviously the children were simply considered worshippers with the adults. Children participated in Passover, the Feast of Weeks, and the Feast of Booths (Ex. 12:3; Deut. 16:11, 14; 1 Sam. 1:4). They also ate of the family peace offerings (Deut. 12:6–7, 11–12, 17–18). The children of priests also ate of the portions they were given from the altar (Lev. 10:14).

For all these special meals one was required to be ceremonially clean. If a mother had to touch one of her children during the time of the month she was menstruating, for example, that child would have to get his clothes washed, he would have to bathe, and would remain unclean until evening (Lev. 15:19–22). To use the language of the author of Hebrews, in the Mosaic covenant, children were washed (Heb. 9:10).

The Promise Fulfilled

When Christ came and established the new covenant, he did not annul his promise to be the God of our children. On the contrary, it is written: "Now they were bringing even infants to him that he might touch them. And when the disciples saw it, they rebuked them. But Jesus called them to him, saying, 'Let the children come to me, and do not hinder them, for to such belongs the kingdom of God. Truly, I say to you, whoever does not receive the kingdom of God like a child shall not enter it' " (Luke 18:15–17).

Notice, first of all, that these are *infants* to whom Jesus is referring. Secondly, their parents had to bring them to Jesus. Thirdly, even though Christian baptism is not instituted, Jesus *does* use the occasion to teach on how one is to "enter" the kingdom. Just as male children were admitted into the covenant by their circumcision, so people now enter the church through baptism (1 Cor. 12:13).

The apostle Peter makes it clear that God's covenant still involves the promise to our children: "For the promise is for you and for your children and for all who are far off, everyone whom the Lord our God calls to himself." (Acts 2:39). We who now profess Christ are among those who are "far off," whom the Lord has called to himself. Just like those to whom Peter first preached, the promise is not only for us but for our children as well.

The apostle Paul also declares that children are included in the covenant. He states that even if one of the parents of a child is an unbeliever, the child is, nevertheless, "holy" (1 Cor. 7:14). If the child does not have the right to be baptized and thereby admitted into the church, what is the point of declaring the child holy? Indeed, Paul tells the Corinthians that Israel was baptized when they crossed the Red Sea—a baptism which included the infants as well as the rest of the Israelites (1 Cor. 10:1–2). Like Peter, Paul's gospel included the children of believers: "Believe in the Lord Jesus, and you will be saved, you and your household" (Acts 16:31).

Children and "Conversion"

There is a widespread notion among Christians that their children, before being baptized, need to be "converted"—to experience a self-conscious time at which one "became" a Christian. As a result, children are not baptized as soon as they can talk and confess "Jesus is Lord," even though the claim is often made that one must merely "profess faith" in order to be baptized. Rather, children are often forced to wait seven to fifteen years before being baptized because it is assumed that they have not truly been "converted."

Besides all the promises and statements of Scripture that I mentioned above, we need to ask ourselves if we really know what we are saying when we demand a conversion experience from our children. What is it that our children need to be converted *from*?

Do They Need to Repent of Refusing to Believe the Gospel?

I have never heard a two-year-old or three-year-old child tell his mommy or daddy that they are wrong when they say that God exists, or that Jesus died for their sins, or that the Holy Spirit lives in our hearts. To tell children that they need to "believe" is a rather strange use of the word. By the grace of God, the young children of Christian parents never know a time when they did not believe the gospel! They need to be encouraged to persevere in their belief and grow up to be mature, godly men and women; they do not need their faith undermined by a parent who claims that they are actually unbelievers who have yet to demonstrate true faith!

Do They Need to Repent of Denying the Gospel by Living in Unrepentant Sin?

Of course, children are sinners, and need to be taught to continually repent and pray for forgiveness when they commit sins, but how can anyone accuse children of living in unrepentant sin? If you accused a professing Christian adult of such a thing, you would need to have evidence or else you would be guilty of gross slander. What did our children ever do to be lumped into the category of "hypocrite," without any evidence whatsoever? Why should they be considered guilty until proven innocent?

Do They Need to Repent of Trying to Save Themselves by Their Own Good Works?

On the one hand, if we teach our children that they are sinners and that God loves them anyway, and sent his Son Jesus to die in their place, why would any child ever think that he could get to heaven by being good enough? On the other hand, if we teach our children that, though they believe and trust in Jesus, they still need to *do* something more in order to go to heaven, aren't we actually teaching them that faith is not enough, but must be supplemented by some sort of additional work?

Do They Need to Reach the "Age of Accountability"?

What Christian parents often seem to forget is that if we say our children are not yet converted, then we are claiming that they are God-haters on their way to hell. There is no other option. Some people have tried to invent a third possibility by claiming that children are not sinners in God's sight until they reach some unknown "age of accountability." This lets them consider their children out of danger until about the time they make a profession of faith.

This idea simply proves that necessity is the mother of invention. The "age of accountability" is believed simply because it is unthinkable to consider one's children enemies of Christ and the Gospel for the first years of their lives. There is no evidence for any such "age" in Scripture before which they are not guilty of sin. On the contrary, there is no point in anyone's existence, no age, no matter how young, when that person is not ethically accountable to God. Either he is a hellbound sinner, or he is saved by grace. He is either in the old Adam, or in the new Adam. If the Holy Spirit has not incorporated our children into Jesus Christ then they are without God and without hope in the world. There are no other options.

Does Any Christian Parent Truly Believe His or Her Children are Unconverted?

Do we not believe that our children are incorporated into Christ? When a child is born to us, do we not rejoice? Do we not teach them to pray the Lord's Prayer, to call God by the name of "Father"? Do we not smile when they learn to sing "Jesus Loves Me"? If our children are unconverted, then all of this is totally wrong. We are simply giving them false confidence. It is blasphemy for an unbeliever to say the Lord's Prayer and call God his "Father." It is presumption for an unregenerate hypocrite to sing "Jesus loves me, this I know, for the Bible tells me so."

When tragedy strikes Christians and a mother miscarries or a toddler dies, do we think that the child is now in hell, or do we trust in God's promise that he is the God not only of ourselves but of our children as well? On Hank Hanegraff's radio show, "Bible Answer Man," I once heard a caller under obvious emotional stress ask about his two-and-a-half-year-old little girl. He was calling on the anniversary of her death in an automobile accident. He said she prayed to Jesus and joyfully sang about him, but he didn't think she had ever knowingly "asked Jesus into her heart." Because of this, the man was unsure that his child was in heaven. He needed to be pointed in the direction of God's promises to his people.

Thank God he has given us firm covenant promises which we can trust! We don't have to suffer the sort of torment which other Christian parents put themselves through because they don't understand the covenant. Let's not undermine these precious promises with any false and shallow ideas about conversion that would deny Christ's blessings to our young children.

Children and Confession

Related to the question as to whether Christian children need conversion, we also need to talk about whether a child's profession of faith is *credible*.

Is a Child's Confession Orthodox?

Of course, sometimes children raised as Christians don't give us the answers that we expect of them. If we ask a four-year-old girl why she would be admitted into heaven, she might say, "Because I go to church," or "because I obey my parents."

Now this may *sound* like the treason of works-righteousness, but do we really understand the child's meaning when we interpret her words in such a way? After all, the only reason we can expect to inherit eternal life is because God, in his great mercy, has promised to give us eternal life. But he has not promised to give eternal life to everyone. Only those who belong to Christ will benefit from what he has done. I often suspect that the child is simply explaining why she thinks she belongs to Christ. She is not explaining the meritorious ground of her justification (the imputed righteousness of Jesus Christ), or the instrument of her justification (faith), but rather she is giving reasons for believing that she is one of God's people to whom the promise of eternal life has been given. And those reasons involve one's membership in God's covenant, the church, and all the fruits which count as evidence that one is truly God's child, including one's obedience to the authorities God has appointed.

In other words, if Jesus asked the four-year-old girl, "Why should I let you into my heaven?" her answer is, "because you promised to let me in." The mention of obedience and church attendance is evidence that the child is among those to whom Christ has made that promise. The Westminster Confession of Faith recognizes this sort of answer because assurance of eternal life is based in part on the presence "of those graces to which the promises are made" (Chapter 18.2).

How should we deal with such confusion? How should we make sure that our children know the difference between a reason for assurance of eternal life and a reason for the meriting of eternal life? Very simply, we should try to explain it in an age-appropriate fashion. If the child says that she gets to go to heaven because she goes to church, we should not be shocked, but simply explain to her that people who go to church get to go to heaven because Jesus died for them. As the child grows and matures, a more elaborate explanation can (and should) be given (one that explains why not all people who go to church will get to heaven).

It is certainly true that a three-year-old believer will confess his faith differently than a thirteen-year-old. And a thirteen-year-old will confess his faith differently than a thirty-three-year-old. As the believer gets older, his confession should become more comprehensive. But where in the Bible does it give us an age at which one's confession is comprehensive enough to count as genuine, and before which it is regarded simply as rote and insincere? We have no more warrant for discounting the confession of a three-year-old than that of a thirteen-year-old, or even a thirty-three-year-old. All three of them could always mature further in the faith and give a more comprehensive confession. If God says that he has prepared praise "out of the mouth of infants and nursing babes" (Matt. 21:16; Ps. 8:2), then we are on rather dangerous ground claiming that the immature confession of faith of a child is not good enough to count as a genuine Christian confession. If we patiently get to know these little ones, we will find that they are believers, even if they can't explain doctrines as well as we would expect from older children.

Is a Child's Confession Sincere?

Another common objection to taking the confession of children as an evidence of genuine Christian faith is that young children will believe or do anything that their parents teach them, and that therefore their profession of faith is not to be regarded as sincere or authentic. But does such an objection make any sense? The reason why children believe whatever their parents teach them is precisely because they are quite capable of sincere faith! Furthermore, the Bible promises that the Holy Spirit is at work in our children (Isa. 59:21). When parents train and discipline their child in the nurture and admonition of the Lord, there is more going on than a purely natural work. We are not simply conditioning our children by rewards and punishments. The Holy Spirit is also at work in our child's heart. This expectation of the Spirit's work in our children should affect how we view our children's faith. When the Bible says that "every spirit that confesses that Jesus Christ has come in the flesh is from God" (1

John 4:2), or that "no one can say Jesus is Lord except by the Holy Spirit (1 Cor. 12:3), no exception is given for children under the age of five.

What About Children Who Grow Up to be Unbelievers?

Finally, the fact that some children grow up and apostatize from the faith is viewed as a reason for us not to take a four-year-old's confession of faith seriously. But this also happens with adults who profess faith. The Bible tells us that Simon the Sorcerer "believed" (Acts 8:13), but then fell away. Jesus told us that some in the church will "believe for a while, and in time of testing fall away" (Luke 8:13). The Bible does not give us some age after which we no longer need to worry about the possibility of apostasy. If we can take the profession of faith of an adult at face value, despite the possibility of apostasy, then there is no reason we should not also take the profession of faith of a child at face value.

How do we deal with the possibility that a child might apostatize in the future? The same way we deal with that possibility for adults. We exhort them to continue in the faith (Col. 1:23) and to grow up and mature as Christians through the means of grace. We exhort them not to receive the grace of God in vain by turning away from the gospel (2 Cor. 6:1), but to hold fast to the Word by which they were saved (1 Cor. 15:2). In other words, we exhort all professing Christians to persevere, but we do not treat people as non-Christians until they achieve some level of commitment that makes them "real" Christians who no longer need to worry about persevering.

How Should We Then Live?

"And when your children say to you, 'What do you mean by this service?' you shall say, 'It is the sacrifice of the Lord's Passover, for he passed over the houses of the people of Israel in Egypt, when he struck the Egyptians but spared our houses' " (Ex. 12:26–27).

"When your son asks you in time to come, 'What is the meaning of the testimonies and the statutes and the rules that the Lord our God has commanded you?' then you shall say to your son, 'We were Pharaoh's slaves in Egypt. And the Lord brought us out of Egypt with a mighty hand. And the Lord showed signs and wonders, great and grievous, against Egypt and against Pharaoh and all his household, before our eyes. And he brought us out from there, that he might bring us in and give us the land that he swore to give to our fathers. And the Lord commanded us to do all these statutes, to fear the Lord our God, for our good always, that he might preserve us alive, as we are this day' " (Deut. 6:20–25).

Here we have two different questions which young children in Israel were expected to ask their parents: What does Passover mean? What does this way of life mean? The answers that the parents were to give in response to these two questions are quite similar to one another. *We do this because God saved us.* That God had delivered Israel was a token of his great love for Israel, which in turn was the basis for Israel's obedience. Moses explains it quite clearly:

> For you are a people holy to the Lord your God. The Lord your God has chosen you to be a people for his treasured possession, out of all the peoples who are on the face of the earth. It was not because you were more in number than any other people that the Lord set his love on you and chose you, for you were the fewest of all peoples, but it is because the Lord loves you and is keeping the oath that he swore to your fathers, that the Lord has brought you out with a mighty hand and redeemed you from the house of slavery, from the hand of Pharaoh king of Egypt.

Know therefore that the Lord your God is God, the faithful God who keeps covenant and steadfast love with those who love him and keep his commandments, to a thousand generations, and repays to their face those who hate him, by destroying them. He will not be slack with one who hates him. He will repay him to his face. You shall therefore be careful to do the commandment and the statutes and the rules that I command you today. (Deut. 7:6–11)

Here again we see the faith of Israel: *God loves us. God saved us. We must be loyal to him; if we are ultimately unfaithful, we will be cut off from his covenant.* This motive is summarized in the beginning of the Ten Commandments: "I am the Lord your God, who brought you out of the land of Egypt, out of the house of slavery. You shall have no other gods before me" (Ex. 20:2–3). Again: *God saved us. We must be loyal to him.*

The Israelites were told to teach their children what God has done for them, and how they should respond in loving trust and grateful obedience. Every Israelite knew that God loved him because God loved Israel and he was a part of Israel. In the case of male children, they were made members of Israel by circumcision. Nevertheless, they knew they would not inherit the promises if they did not persevere in faith. We see this same pattern in the teaching of Jesus, when he told the disciples:

> I am the true vine, and my Father is the vine-dresser. Every branch in me that does not bear fruit he takes away, and every branch that does bear fruit he prunes, that it may bear more fruit. Already you are clean because of the word that I have spoken to you. Abide in me, and I in you. As the branch cannot bear fruit by itself, unless it abides in the vine, neither can you, unless you abide in me. I am the vine; you are the branches. Whoever abides in me and I in him, he it is that bears much fruit, for apart from me you can do nothing. If anyone does not abide in me he is thrown away like a branch and withers; and the branches are gathered, thrown into the fire, and burned. If you abide in me, and my words abide in you, ask whatever you wish, and it will be done for you. By this my Father is glorified, that you bear much fruit and so prove to be my disciples. As the Father has loved me, so have I loved you. Abide in my love. (John 15:1–9)

Jesus gives his disciples a similar motivation to that which he gaves to Old Testament Israel through Moses: *Jesus loves us. Jesus saved us. We must be loyal to him.* Jesus gave himself for his bride, the church (Eph. 5:25).

Just like the deliverance of Israel from Egypt, Christ's victory over Satan and death through his crucifixion and resurrection is an objective historical fact. It is the object of faith for all Christians and the surety of the promises Christ has made for the future.

We are told to teach our children what God has done for them and how they should respond in loving trust and grateful obedience. Every Christian should know that God loves him because God loves his bride, the church, and the Christian is a part of the church. We have all been made members of the church through baptism. Nevertheless, we know we will not inherit the promises if we do not persevere in faith.

A Christian philosophy of raising children should be based on our objective standing in Christ's kingdom, conferred on us and our children through baptism. According to Deuteronomy 6:20–25, when our children ask us about why we do certain things or don't do certain things, we should tell them about what Jesus has done for: how he died for us and rose again and sent his Spirit to give his church union and communion with himself. How he providentially arranged for us to be made members of his church through baptism, and how he weekly renews his covenant with us—meets with us, forgives our sins, and feeds us with himself. How we must respond to his great love and wonderful promises by believing them with a trusting heart, and by responding in grateful obedience all our lives.

The only way we can expect any child to have a firm faith is by giving him a firm foundation on which that faith may rest. If we make our children think that God's favor in Christ is something that they need to attain, then we will greatly confuse them. Instead, we must teach them that they have been engrafted into Christ (Rom. 11:17) by his great mercy to them. We must raise them to respond to God's love and mercy in Christ by a life of faith and obedience, so that they remain in him and he in them (John 15:4).

Let us not cause our children to stumble by keeping them outside the church. Let us rather welcome them into the church by baptism and build them up in the faith that they may inherit eternal life.

The Relationship Between Covenant Membership and Salvation

To be in covenant with God is to be his child, have his name placed upon you, and to walk with him. In short, it is the fullness of the Christian life.

Perhaps you're not convinced yet. Perhaps you are concerned about those children who grow up to be unbelievers. Was this because the parents or the church failed to properly encourage their "conversion"? How does the Bible deal with those who may not actually believe the gospel in a "saving" way?

The sad truth is that not everyone who enters into covenant with God inherits eternal life. Some "believe for a while" (Luke 8:13) but fall away. Jesus warned the Jews of his day that "sons of the kingdom will be thrown into the outer darkness" (Matt. 8:12). Of those who are Jesus's disciples, ". . . the one who endures to the end will be saved" (Matt. 10:22).

What we see in the Bible generally are strong, gracious encouragements to a confident living-out of God's love, but when there is the need to deal with the possibility of unbelief, then the Bible shows us gracious warnings not to throw the love of God away. Grab your Bible and consider the following passages.

Romans 11:17–24

Since chapter nine, Paul has been explaining the apostasy of Israel, showing that "they are not all Israel, who are from Israel." Not all were regenerated by the Spirit so that they would continually live by faith and demonstrate this by recognizing Jesus as the Messiah. Nevertheless, all *were* objectively members of God's covenant people: "to them belong the adoption, the glory, the covenants, the giving of the law, the worship, and the promises" (Rom. 9:4). However, the covenant is conditional upon perseverance in faith: "For circumcision indeed is of value if you obey the law, but if you break the law, your circumcision becomes uncircumcision" (Rom. 2:25). Thus, only those truly regenerated by the Spirit so that they are faithful to the end show themselves to be true Israelites.

Paul is concerned that the Gentile converts might become presumptuous and arrogant because of Jewish apostasy. Thus, he presents them with a severe warning, which applies to us as well. Just because you "were grafted in among the others and now share in the nourishing root of the olive tree" (Rom. 11:17b) does not mean that you have no need to fear God's covenant curse. On the contrary, you will only inherit eternal life "provided you continue in his kindness. Otherwise you too will be cut off " (Rom. 11:22b).

1 Corinthians 9:24–10:12

Here we have a warning given to the Corinthians based on the negative example of the Israelites in the wilderness. All the Israelites saved from Egypt were baptized into Moses, ate spiritual food, and drank spiritual water from Christ himself, but the Israelites did not persevere in what they had been given. Rather they apostatized and fell under the wrath of God. We must be warned by the Old Testament example and make sure we persevere in the faith, lest we likewise perish as covenant breakers.

Paul postulates no distinction between an *identifiable* class of "nominal believers" who are supposed to heed the warning of the Old Testament by being "truly converted" and a class of "true believers" who can simply assume they are never in danger of becoming apostate. On the contrary, Paul concludes with a general rule for all, ". . . let anyone who thinks that he stands take heed lest he fall" (1 Cor. 10:12), after beginning with the example of *himself*: "But I discipline my body and keep it under control, lest after preaching to others I myself should be disqualified" (1 Cor. 9:27). Paul makes it clear that he, no less than the Corinthians, must heed the warning of the Old Testament.

Colossians 1:21–23a

Here we have the plainest statement possible: that the new covenant is a conditional covenant. If one is to be revealed as the recipient of Christ's imputed righteousness on the Day of Judgment, one must persevere in the faith. The strongest language conceivable is used to describe Christ's covenant relationship with the Colossians: "And you, who once were alienated and hostile in mind, doing evil deeds, he has now reconciled in his body of flesh by his death, in order to present you holy and blameless and above reproach before him" (Col. 1:21–22).

Any thought that the Colossians can continue to be confident of their eternal salvation apart from continuing in faith is forcefully removed. They will only be presented "holy and blameless and beyond reproach" before God, "if indeed you continue in the faith, stable and steadfast, not shifting from the hope of the gospel that you heard" (Col. 1:23a).

Notice there is no desire on Paul's part to somehow throw doubt on the reality of their initiation in the covenant of grace. He doesn't throw doubt on the grace they have objectively received but only exhorts them to continue in it. (Those who continue will demonstrate that they are truly regenerate and chosen by God to inherit eternal life; those who rebel against God will demonstrate that they are not elect.)

Hebrews 3–4

The author of Hebrews here addresses "you who share in a heavenly calling" (Heb. 3:1). Furthermore, he includes himself in the exhortations ("Let us therefore strive to enter that rest" [Heb. 4:11]). His entire message is parallel to 1 Corinthians 10:1–13, for he compares the Christians receiving the letter to those with whom God made a covenant in the wilderness but who failed to enter the land because of unbelief. They have been initiated in the covenant of grace and now they must continue in it.

Notice that the author of Hebrews exhorts his readers to endure because they have Christ as a sympathetic high priest (Heb. 4:14–16). Obviously, if they do not endure, the fault is all the more with them, because they have spurned such a gracious God. The author doesn't say that some have access to this priest but that others don't. No, it is perfectly plain—and made even more and more evident, if that were possible, by almost every other chapter in Hebrews—that those who fall away are guilty of having spurned their high priest and have refused to "draw near to the throne of grace, that we may receive mercy and find grace to help in time of need" (Heb. 4:16).

While I certainly think the author of Hebrews believed in a qualitative difference between the faith of those whose faith was predestined to endure and the faith of those who were going to fall away, he doesn't seem to think it is worth mentioning. He simply exhorts all professing Christians to "hold our original confidence firm to the end" (Heb. 3:14), to "hold fast our confession" (Heb. 4:14). On the contrary, "unbelief" (Heb. 3:19) is identified with "disobedience" (Heb. 4:6; 3:18) on the part of those who have been engrafted into the covenant of grace. The objective standing of the readers in Christ's new covenant is not any more in doubt than the membership of the wilderness generation in the Mosaic covenant. What is in doubt is whether they are going to enter God's rest. This will not happen unless they persevere. If they become "hardened by the deceitfulness of sin" (Heb. 3:13) then they will provoke God to wrath. No matter what sort of belief they once possessed, it will only count as unbelief if they fall away from the living God (cf. Eze. 18:24). Remember, "fall[ing] away from the living God" (Heb. 3:12) presupposes standing in covenant relation with him.

Hebrews 10:4–39

Here we find the author of Hebrews presenting huge contrasts between the Mosaic covenant and the new covenant. But there is a particular similarity between the periods in the covenant of grace both preceding and following Christ. Under both administrations of the covenant, some do not persevere but rebel against God despite his great blessings. As covenant breakers, such people fall under God's covenantal wrath.

Even here, however, we do find a significant contrast: those who break the new covenant are to be much more severely punished than those who merely broke the Mosaic covenant. "Anyone who has set aside the law of Moses dies without mercy on the evidence of two or three witnesses. How much worse punishment, do you think, will be deserved by the one who has spurned the Son of God, and has profaned the blood of the covenant by which he was sanctified, and has outraged the Spirit of grace?" (Heb. 10:28–29).

The author of Hebrews could not be more explicit that he is addressing a singular group of people, members of the new covenant, who all need to continue in what they have been given if they would be saved. "By that will we *have been sanctified* through the offering of the body of Jesus Christ once for all" (Heb. 10:10). And again, "For *by a single offering* he has perfected for all time those *who are being sanctified*" (Heb. 10:14). This same language begins and ends Hebrews: "For he who sanctifies and those *who are sanctified* all have one source. That is why he is not ashamed to call them brothers" (Heb. 2:11). And again: "So Jesus also suffered outside the gate *in order to sanctify the people through his own blood*" (Heb. 13:12). This is exactly the same gift which makes the treason of apostasy such a high-handed sin: "How much worse punishment, do you think, will be deserved by the one who has spurned the Son of God, and has profaned *the blood of the covenant by which he was sanctified*, and has outraged the Spirit of grace?" (Heb. 10:29).

Additionally, the writer of Hebrews makes it clear that all to whom he is writing have privileges—privileges that were purchased at a great price and the despising of which will bring great wrath. "Therefore, brothers, since *we have confidence* to enter the holy places by the blood of Jesus, by the new and living way that he opened for us through the curtain, that is, through his flesh, and *since we have a great priest* over the house of God, *let us draw near* with a true heart in full assurance of faith, with *our hearts sprinkled clean* from an evil conscience and *our bodies washed* with pure water" (Heb. 10:19–22).

All the intended readers share in the same confidence, the same priest, their hearts are all sprinkled and their bodies all washed so that all must draw near, holding fast their "confession of . . . hope without wavering" (10:23), lest any one of them come under the fearful wrath of God.

Again, verses thirty-two and following make it clear that the intended audience consists of people who have made a good start in accepting "joyfully the plundering of [their] property" (Heb. 10:34) but who must "not throw away [their] confidence, which has a great reward" (Heb. 10:35). The Pauline prooftext for justification by faith alone is used to demonstrate that "endurance" in faith is required for us to "receive what is promised" (Heb. 10:36). The writer of Hebrews expresses confidence that his readers will endure in such faith to the preserving of the soul (Heb. 10:39).

Conclusion

All these passages have been mentioned (and many more could be cited) to defend the integrity of God's covenant. All professing believers and their children belong to God and should be brought into covenant relation to him in baptism, the ritual of admission into his church. I have no doubt that God adopts and cares for believers and their children who, through ignorance, faulty teaching, or some other hindrance, are kept from baptism. But the Bible teaches that God wants and has a visible society or family on the earth that is marked out, among other things, by an induction ceremony.

Though it is true that some people who enter into God's covenant community, the church, do not persevere in the faith and end up "fall[ing] away from the living God" (Heb. 3:12), they could not fall away unless they were first elevated into covenant fellowship with God. The fact that some abandon the covenant does not mean that they were never in the covenant, because otherwise there would be nothing for them to abandon.

Thus, all professing Christians have been engrafted into the covenant and must continue in it (John 15:1ff). All alike must endure to the end if they would be saved (Matt. 10:22). The abstract possibility that someone might later apostatize from the faith does not give us any biblical warrant to doubt whether they are fellow members of the covenant. The Bible simply declares that all professing Christians have received the grace of God and, if necessary, exhorts them "not to receive the grace of God in vain" (2 Cor. 6:1).

Please bear in mind that warnings are actually not the emphasis in the New Covenant situation, but rather believers and their children are encouraged with positive promises. "In Christ Jesus you are all sons of God, through faith," writes the Apostle Paul, "For as many of you as were baptized into Christ have put on Christ . . . And if you are Christ's, then you are Abraham's offspring, heirs according to promise." Baptism is a source of encouragement that we might trust God to fulfill all his promises to us.

Why baptize babies? Because we want to assure our children all through their lives, as we raise them to follow and trust Jesus, that, through the ministry of his church, God has taken possession of them as members of his very own family.

Appendix:
The Covenant Meal

Perhaps you're *still* not convinced. Even if we concede our children belong to God, does this mean they ought to be baptized? Where is the precedent for applying water to children in the name of the Lord?

The fact is that there is plenty of precedent if one knows where to look. God has not merely implied but has explicitly said that he wants to eat and drink with our children as much as he wants to eat and drink with us. And, just as in our own homes, God tells us to "wash up" before dinner.

God's covenant is especially celebrated and re-established by a regular meal with him. This began in the Garden of Eden with the Tree of Life. It continued in the Abrahamic covenant when food was served for covenantal fellowship between God and man, and between man and man (Gen. 14:18; 18:1–8; 26:26–33). In the Mosaic covenant, the people were given communion with God by eating from the altar (1 Cor. 10:18; cf. Lev. 10:14; 17:1–7; 21:22; Deut. 21:11–12, 17–19, 27; 16:1–17). Finally, fellowship with God and communion with Christ in the new covenant is especially renewed and strengthened in the Lord's Supper (1 Cor. 10:15–22).

It will be helpful to point out here that the sacred meals in which the Israelites participated were symbolically tied to the Tree of Life. Moses forbade the people of God from participating in the sacraments anywhere except "before the Lord your God in the place where the Lord your God will choose" (Deut. 12:18), that is, "at the place which the Lord your God shall choose from all your tribes, to establish his name there for his dwelling" (Deut. 12:5). This place of fellowship was first the tabernacle, and then the temple Solomon built. In both cases, this sanctuary was, among other things, a new Garden of Eden. The tabernacle contained a Tree of Light—a lampstand stylized as an almond tree that was always in season (Ex. 25:31–37). Interwoven in the veil of the tabernacle were cherubim guarding the inner sanctuary (Ex. 26:31). In the case of Solomon's temple, the architect "carved engraved figures of cherubim and palm trees and open flowers, in the inner and outer rooms" (1 Kings 6:29). Now the implication would be obvious to the Israelites: just as God put a sanctuary Garden in the land of Eden, so he had given them a sanctuary in Israel. After Adam fell, cherubim guarded the Garden, and both the tabernacle and temple were designed to show that they were the continuation of that sanctuary. Thus, eating at the sanctuary was inescapably connected to the food in the Garden of Eden.

This helps us see how much more privileged we are today. Instead of having to migrate only three times a year to a central sanctuary many miles away, we are given access to communion with Christ wherever we gather as a church. Christ, our Tree of Life, has come to us.

He comes to us in a tangible way. Remember, the Bible does not say that Adam and Eve enjoyed some sort of intangible, "spiritual," immaterial communion with God—that only after they fell from grace were they given a "symbolic" meal. On the contrary, when they sinned, their fall meant that they lost access to the Tree of Life and were, as a *punishment* for their sin, reduced to an intangible relationship with the Lord. Also remember that the Bible does not say that the sacred meals of Israel were some sort of carnal observance which passed away when Christ came. On the contrary, Jesus gave the church a communion meal which, because it is much simpler and can be done wherever the church meets together, can be observed much more frequently than the three annual feasts of the old covenant.

After all, Jesus *could* have commanded each of us to get alone by ourselves at least once a week, close our eyes, fold our legs into the lotus position, and empty our minds so that we could experience the transcendence of God. He could have commanded us to re-read one of the gospel accounts of his crucifixion and meditate on his suffering in order to stimulate ourselves to more humble gratitude for what Christ did for us. Instead, he established a covenant meal in continuity with the festal celebrations of the old covenant. Doesn't Christ's appointment of a feast tell us something about the nature of the kingdom of God and the new covenant?

Christ's communion with his church is not some sort of mental telepathy that takes place apart from symbols. On the contrary, the church communicates with Christ in *words*—prayers and hymns—and of gestures—bowing our heads to show respect, perhaps even lifting up our hands in prayer the way we are commanded to do it in Scripture (1 Tim. 2:8). And Christ also communicates with the church verbally—through the Bible and especially the preaching of the Bible—and non-verbally, through the sacraments.

Thus, while it is true that the kingdom of God is now spiritual, it is not true that the kingdom is *immaterial*. Biblically, something is spiritual because the Holy Spirit gives it. If the kingdom were immaterial then we would not be saved because we are material creatures and sin affects us in a material way. Jesus made it quite clear to Peter that the blessings of the kingdom applied to this age as well as the next. Jesus said, "Truly, I say to you, there is no one who has left house or brothers or sisters or mother or father or children or lands, for my sake and for the gospel, who will not receive a hundredfold now in this time, houses and brothers and sisters and mothers and children and lands, with persecutions, and in the age to come eternal life" (Mark 10:29–30).

The apostle Paul also affirms that the kingdom involves physical blessings. "Children, obey your parents in the Lord, for this is right. 'Honor your father and mother' (this is the first commandment with a promise), that it may go well with you and that you may live long in the land" (Eph. 6:1–3). Paul is quoting the fifth commandment here and explicitly emphasizing the promise of long life. Furthermore, though the original blessing was promised "in the land which the Lord your God gives you" (Ex. 20:12), Paul paraphrases it so that the children he is writing to realize that the blessing now applies everywhere, including Ephesus. The kingdom is no longer reduced to the "physical" nation of Israel but now encompasses *all* the nations of the physical planet. Every time we partake of the Lord's Supper, we are affirming that the kingdom is a tangible reality and that our covenant relationship with God is not some sort of invisible, unspoken, informal relationship, but a real relationship involving both informal and formal means of communication that are both verbal and non-verbal. The church is just as much a tangible reality as the nation of Israel once was. It is spiritual because the Spirit is the one who gives us this tangible, objectively-apprehensible kingdom and makes us a part of it.

As we mentioned above, if Adam had not fallen, he and his posterity would have always had access to the Garden and the Tree of Life within. However, having been banished from the Garden, they could no longer come and go as they pleased. One had to be graciously given access to the feast if one was not to incur God's wrath by trespassing as a sinner into his holy presence.

Access to the Feast in the Mosaic Covenant

From the time of the Exodus, we find God graciously giving people access to the sacramental meals by setting forth sacraments of initiation and cleansing. Thus, to participate in Passover, one must be circumcised—and thus become an Israelite (Ex. 12:43–49). To participate in any of the other sanctuary meals, whether Jew or Gentile (Lev. 17:8; 22:18–25; Num. 15:11–16), one must be ritually cleansed (Lev. 7:20–21; 22:3–7;

Num. 19:13). A person could become unclean in a variety of ways and would need to be cleansed. These cleansings involved various washings with water. Once a person was clean, he or she was able to participate in sanctuary meals. Cleansings restored access to the feasts—access that had been lost due to uncleanness.

There were various kinds of uncleanness and cleansings. If a person touched a corpse, he had to be sprinkled with water mixed with the ashes of a heifer on the third and seventh day (Num. 19). Other cleansings involved washing oneself and one's clothes and then waiting for the evening sacrifice so that one would be clean (Lev. 15:5; cf. Ex. 29:38–41). In the case of one whose flesh was exposed by leprosy, a live bird was dipped in the blood of a sacrificed bird and it was sprinkled over the leper seven times (Lev. 14:1–9).

Interestingly, circumcision and cleansing are actually associated with the laws of Moses. When a woman gave birth to a girl, she was unclean for two weeks plus sixty-six days (Lev. 12:5). However, when a woman had a male child, then the two weeks of uncleanness were cut in half, followed by the child's circumcision on the eighth day (Lev. 12:2–3). Afterward, she was only unclean for thirty-three days (v. 4). Circumcision provided cleansing.

There are probably other rites in the Mosaic covenant that also correspond to the initiation of circumcision and/or the re-initiation of cleansing. An Israelite could only marry a woman captured from an enemy nation after she shaved her head, trimmed her nails, removed her old clothes, and waited a month (Deut. 21:10–13). Afterward, she was not a second-class citizen but a free woman (Deut. 21:14). It is not hard to see that this cutting of hair and nails is a symbolic purging of the old in order that a new status might be conferred upon the woman, just as in circumcision the flesh is mortified. We could make similar observations about the requirements for a Nazirite, or the various anointings in the Old Testament. Even these lesser "circumcisions" are associated with cleansing, since the leper also had to shave his head as part of his cleansing ritual (Lev. 14:8).

Again, the most important point is that various forms of uncleanness barred one from approaching God in his sanctuary and participating in the sanctuary meals. Cleansing, in whatever way it was done, gave one access to the sanctuary meals. Once cleansed, you could have fellowship with God through food.

Access in the New Covenant

With the coming and work of Jesus, the ceremonies of the Mosaic law were superseded. Jesus instituted a new covenant with new and much simpler ceremonies.

To repeat what was pointed out before, the New Covenant is not entirely without any ceremonies or rituals. On the contrary, Jesus clearly instructed us to baptize and to partake of bread and wine in the Lord's Supper. These rites are much simpler than their many Old Covenant counterparts. Nevertheless, it is unbiblical and un-Christian to claim that we no longer have any ceremonies in the church.

All the feasts of the Mosaic covenant are fulfilled in the Lord's Supper (1 Cor. 10:3–4, 18). In eating and drinking we share in the body and blood of Christ (1 Cor. 10:17) and have fellowship with him by the power of the Holy Spirit. It is easy to see, then, that baptism corresponds to the cleansings of the Mosaic covenant and fulfills them. This is declared in Hebrews 9:10 where the ceremonial washings are called "baptisms" (literal translation from the Greek). Furthermore, just as circumcision was associated with cleansing in the Mosaic covenant, so baptism is associated with circumcision in the new covenant and is said to supersede it (Col. 2:9–12; cf. Gal. 3:26–29).

Thus, all the various types of rites and ceremonies in the Old Covenant are fulfilled in two simple rituals—baptism and the Lord's Supper. These correspond to the two major classifications of rituals in the Mosaic covenant—all the circumcisions and cleansing on the one hand, and all the sacrificial meals on the other.

Now, instead of needing to be "baptized" over and over again in order to gain access to the sanctuary meals, baptism is performed once and for all. Instead of baptism involving blood or the ashes of a heifer, now baptism requires nothing more than water and the Word. Because Christ offered himself up to die a bloody death on Calvary two thousand years ago, there is no longer any place for bloody rites. Nor do we have to deal with sin and death over and over again. One baptism is sufficient to give us access to the feast forever and ever.

God is the One Who Gives Access

The New Testament never speaks of baptism as something that someone does to himself. The command is always to "be baptized," never to "baptize yourself" (Mark 16:16; Acts 2:38; 22:16). While the command to the *evangelized* is to be baptized, the command to the *evangelists* is to baptize (Matt 28:19). Those who are baptized are said to be "added" to the church

(Acts 2:41). Baptism signifies being united to Christ (Rom. 6:3–11), being clothed with Christ so that one belongs to him (Gal. 3:27–29), being circumcised "without hands" and "made alive together with" Christ (Col. 2:11–13). Obviously, all these things are impossible for us. God must do them.

Paul also tells the Corinthians that they were baptized by the Spirit (1 Cor. 12:13). He tells the Ephesians that Christ "cleansed" the church "by the washing of water with the word" (Eph. 5:26); almost certainly a reference to baptism in the name of the Holy Trinity. The person who baptizes does so as God's representative. We are not baptized by men, but by God working through his representatives.

The point here is that nowhere in Scripture is baptism treated as a testimony or symbol of a person's faith. On the contrary, baptism is a sign of *God's* sovereign act in making us members of his church. Baptism is not a seal of "works done by us in righteousness," but rather of the "renewal of the Holy Spirit, whom he [God our Savior] poured out on us richly through Jesus Christ our Savior" (Titus 3:4–6).